Effective Strategies for Teaching Minority Students

by
Howard D. Hill

National Educational Service
Bloomington, Indiana

TABLE OF CONTENTS

About the Author

Howard D. Hill received the Ph.D. degree in Curriculum and Instruction at Kansas State University, Manhattan, Kansas. He is a former secondary social studies teacher, supervisor of instruction, and assistant principal in the public schools of Arkansas and Mississippi. Hill has held a number of appointments at colleges and universities across the United States. From 1979 to 1987, he was professor and chairman of the Department of Education at South Carolina State College, Orangeburg, S.C. He has published widely in professional journals. His interest in the crucial area of minority education was sparked during the time he was completing research for his doctoral dissertation, "A Descriptive Study of Unwed Parenthood Among Secondary School-Age Students and the Implications for Curriculum Revision in the Cognitive/Affective Domain" (1973). A member of the executive board of the Association of Teacher Educators, he currently is the director of chapter programs at Phi Delta Kappa International in Bloomington, Indiana.

Dedication

To the teachers, school administrators, and parents throughout the country who believe that minority students are capable of learning and succeeding in school.

Foreword

In 1986, the population of the United States was approximately 240 million, with 21 percent — approximately 50 million — comprised of Asians, Hispanics, and Blacks. According to the federal government, one out of every three Americans will be "minority" members soon after the beginning of the twenty-first century. Thus, the nation's racial composition is changing significantly.

Webster's Dictionary defines "minority" as the smaller in number of two groups constituting a whole. In the history of the U.S., minority groups have traditionally been considered to be comprised of non-Anglo Saxon members of the population. While this situation is rapidly changing and a number of different definitions currently abound, for the purposes of this book the term "minority" will refer to non-white racial and ethnic groups.

It is expected that the population of the United States may be as high as 270 million by the year 2025, with the growth of minority populations a major factor in this population increase.

At the beginning of the 1980s, approximately 28 percent of public school students were minority members. There now are three states where "minorities" constitute majority enrollment (Mississippi, Hawaii, and California). In the nation's largest school systems, the majority of the students are a "minority." These demographics must be taken into account in the development and implementation of educational programs.

The quality of education in schools attended predominantly by minority students is getting *progressively worse.* This is substantiated by the following: 1) there is a great disparity between minority and non-minority students' test scores; 2) teachers are becoming "educational custodians" rather than facilitators of knowledge; 3) the "white flight" phenomenon has created hardships for inner-city schools in generating the capital needed to adequately finance education; 4) many teachers lack classroom management skills vital to successful teaching of minority students; and 5) there is decreasing number of competent minority teachers entering the education profession.

Educators believe that teacher training institutions do not adequately prepare prospective teachers of educationally underprepared minority students. Often teacher training programs emphasize methodologies that are not well suited to handling the challenges presented by minority students.

Teachers who enter the profession of education in the 1990s and beyond must be prepared to teach minority students. Many will not have the choice of deciding whether they will teach in the suburbs or in inner-city schools with large minority student populations.

H.D.H.

Acknowledgments

Inspiration for this book came from several quarters. First, I thank Alan Blankstein for approaching me with the idea for this book and for his encouragement.

The production of a book requires the efforts of many; therefore, my sincere thanks also goes to the editorial staff at National Educational Service (NES) in Bloomington, Indiana, and to Nancy R. Shin, Director of Operations for NES.

I would like to extend special thanks to those persons who, directly or indirectly, influenced my thinking on the topics that are found in these pages. These include graduate students at the University of Houston-University Park and South Carolina State College, Orangeburg.

Finally I would like to acknowledge the support of my family for their individual and collective contribution to this effort, including my wife, Clemmie; my son and daughter, Ray and Edith; and my parents, Della Mae and Howard Hill, Jr. Thank you all — you were wonderful in many ways during the production of this book.

Introduction

Teachers increasingly find themselves in a classroom environment that is not conducive to effective teaching or real learning. This is especially true for teachers in schools where minority students are in the majority. It was recently shown in a major survey that minority teachers are experiencing "burnout" in teaching.[1]

Many teachers have little or no experience with the educational needs or culture of minorities. The training of prospective and inservice teachers generally has not included the necessary courses and hands-on experience to facilitate understanding the environment where these students live and go to school. Since teachers who work in schools with minority students often do not live in these communities, their knowledge about the lifestyle of their students tends to be limited.

In addition, a large percentage of practicing teachers have not had courses in urban education or multicultural studies. Thus, there is a strong need for special publications for teachers who find themselves teaching minority students but are unsure how best to meet their needs.

Effective Strategies for Teaching Minority Students attempts to fill some of the voids in the prospective teacher's (and veteran teacher's) repertoire of skills. Included are recommendations for practical applications of theory in the classroom.

Effective Strategies for Teaching Minority Students is designed to provide an overview of many issues that are essential in understanding, relating to, and, ultimately, teaching minority students. The recommendations for interacting with minority students are based both on research and personal classroom experiences. The book is presented in a practical, easy-to-read format. The chapters are succinct and references to the plethora of research that went into writing the publication have been kept to a minimum. This book is recommended for preservice and inservice teachers and anyone interested in education in communities where minority students make up a sizeable portion of the school enrollment.

---

1. "In Teacher Poll, Minorities Show Signs of Distress," *Education Week,* October 5, 1988, p. 1.

In the following pages I offer nothing more than simple facts, plain arguments and common sense; and have no other preliminaries to settle with the reader, other than that he will divest himself of prejudice and prepossession, and suffer his reason and his feelings to determine for themselves; that he will put on, or rather that he will not put off, the true character of a man, and generously enlarge his views beyond the present.

Thomas Paine, *Common Sense*

Chapter 1
Requisite Preparation for Teachers of Minority Students

> *If a doctor, lawyer, or dentist had 40 people in his office at one time, all of whom had different needs, and some of whom didn't want to be there and were causing trouble, and the doctor, lawyer, or dentist, without assistance, had to treat them all with professional excellence for nine months, then he might have some conception of the classroom teacher's job.*
>
> Donald O. Quinn

1988 was an Olympic year. For this international event, no country sends its players into the international spotlight without ensuring that their talents are honed for exemplary performance. That is the nature of the Olympics: prepare well and excel to the fullest extent possible.

1988 was also a time when many beginning and veteran teachers were given teaching assignments in schools where minority students are in the majority. Unlike the players in the Olympics, a large percentage of these teachers entered the schools without the benefit of proper training and conditioning. In effect, they were not fit to perform or meet the myriad of classroom challenges that awaited them.

This is precisely what has been happening in America's schools for years. Teachers who generally have the least training for teaching difficult students are sent to the most difficult schools. Should this continue to be the case? Are these teaching assignments symptomatic of why so many ills exist in the schools today? What are the requisite skills and attitudes teachers of minority students must display?

It would be unwise for a teacher to accept a teaching assignment in a school setting in which he or she lacks familiarity. Yet teachers lacking skills in teaching certain segments of the student population often are licensed by a state department of education to teach those students. Such is the case for beginning teachers and for those more experienced teachers who do not have adequate preparation for teaching educationally underprepared students.

There is a basic preparation that all teachers should have. But for those teachers entering schools comprised heavily of minority students, more than minimal preparation is necessary; they need essential preparation. It has been said that "To teach is to learn twice."

Be prepared to teach educationally underprepared students. A large percentage of minority students are educationally underprepared. This means that you may have to develop skills to handle compensatory, remedial, and developmental learning needs. However, be mindful that educationally underprepared minority students show as wide a range in learning ability as any other group. In fact, many will eventually receive scholarships to Yale, Berkeley, Michigan, Harvard, Hampton, and other excellent institutions.

Develop a second language skill. It is very helpful for a teacher to be able to speak a second (or third) language. Spanish is of value to all teachers. An understanding of regional dialects and slang is also helpful. Well-developed and varied language skills are at the heart of the communication process with students.

Develop street smarts. Know what ribbin'[1], jivin'[2], and playin' the dozens[3] are about. These games eventually come up in the classroom, corridors, cafeteria, and elsewhere at school. Teachers must play tough, because otherwise these games can be psychologically devastating. Such games are especially hard on the non-minority teacher who may be the only one in the classroom unaware of or unable to understand a remark that has been made to him or her by a student.

Be aware of cultural and ethnic history. It is imperative that teachers be knowledgeable about the cultural and ethnic history of all minority students in their classroom. If in-depth information of this kind is not yet known, the teacher must acquire it quickly. Important historical dates must be understood and recognized by the teacher and, where possible, celebrated.

Ethnic literature must be used in teaching whenever possible. References can be made to minorities and their many contributions to education, the arts, music, literature, the sciences, and other facets of life. Teachers should be sure to include materials relevant to the minority groups they are teaching as a necessary balance to the regular curriculum.

Intercultural differences or idiosyncrasies must be examined and understood. For instance, some people believe that using CPT (Colored People Time) in reference to Black Americans involves stereotyping and should be avoided. Regardless of this, the acronym does have meaning which can be helpful. (Its implied message is that if school is scheduled to start at 8:15 a.m., students will arrive at 8:45 a.m., 9:00 a.m., or even later.) Ethnic differences of this kind must be understood by teachers of minority students.

It is expected that teachers of minority students will have completed *formal courses in urban education and multicultural understanding* during their initial teacher certification program or, if not then, as requirements for a master's degree. If such courses are not completed, a serious void will exist in the teacher's academic background.

Find a mentor. If you know someone with success in teaching minority students, let that person know that you need assistance. When a genuine friendship with someone is established before mentoring begins, the likelihood is greatest that favorable results will be realized and students will benefit. A teacher's race does not determine his success in classrooms where minority students constitute the largest enrollment. There are cases on record where non-minority teachers have had greater success in teaching minority students than have minority teachers. What is essential to teaching success with minority students is that the teacher 1) be academically competent, 2) be personable but not overly friendly, and 3) have a considerable repertoire of teaching methods at his or her disposal.

These are some of the requisite skills, attitudes, and behaviors teachers need to exercise prior to and during their engagements with minority students. There are others that also are important for teachers to consider. What is most essential, however, is that teachers truly believe they can teach minority students effectively. In this regard, they must reign as true professionals do: stand tall, put on the armor, walk into the classroom, and announce for one and all to hear, "Let the class begin!"

1. Ribbin' (or ribbing) is to poke fun at.

2. Jivin' is a verbal and physical technique some black students use to avoid difficult situations; to accommodate authority figures; and, to some extent, to prevent themselves from being physically or psychologically abused.

3. Playin' the dozens refers to verbal sparring in which the players trade insults.

Go forward, straight ahead.
There are no limits on your life
but those barricades you build yourself.

Rod McKuen

Chapter 2
Student Success in School and Life

Education must not simply teach work . . .
it must teach life.

W.E.B. Du Bois

Is it possible for most students to be successful in school? Can schools develop programs that are relevant to their needs? What is meant by success in school for a large percentage of students who are poor, underprivileged, and from minority backgrounds?

Christine E. Sleeter and Carl A. Grant effectively stated their views on what success in school and life must be for minority students:

> In essence, we mean that young people leave school empowered to take charge of their own destinies, in a society in which the destinies of many have been characterized by failure, poverty, and despair. For this to happen, the skills and content taught in schools must be broadened.[1]

Sleeter and Grant that school programs must offer minority students the opportunity to grow and expand their horizons. Because of the society in which minority students live, the school must do a much better job of preparing them for the conflicts in life — such as racism that they might encounter. Minority students face many difficulties that non-minority students do not.

Teachers must continue to refine and develop programs that, to a very substantial degree, have an impact on student progress in school and in life. This is important because U.S. society does not give every child an equal chance to live the good life. Even when their level

7

of educational attainment is identical, some youngsters move into positions of power and wealth on leaving school while others lead lives marked by powerlessness. This is the case because society distributes its resources, at least in part, on the basis of race, socioeconomic background, and gender.[2]

The Hispanic Policy Development Project in 1988 found that the dropout rate of Hispanic students can be reduced if educators become more sensitive to such students' need for income. Because 41 percent of Hispanic students who leave school prior to graduation do so for economic reasons, programs targeting the needs of Hispanic dropouts, their families, and their communities will have to be developed. The Hispanic population is largely concentrated in the metropolitan regions of four states: California, Florida, Texas, and New York.

Specifically, the report recommends that middle schools and high schools be restructured to provide opportunities for Hispanic youth to earn wages while they continue their education. It is believed that Hispanic youth who combine school and work will develop greater self-confidence about themselves and their worth as human beings.[3]

When minority students leave school, at whatever point in their lives, their education must be sufficient to help them gain a positive sense of destiny for themselves. This sense of destiny includes:

1. A desire to continue educational training beyond high school.
2. A commitment to maintain good health practices.
3. A better than average awareness of democracy and democratic principles by which to live in the United States.
4. A motivation to succeed in life.

Minority students, at least as much as any other group in the U.S., need to succeed in school. Their failure to meet expectations will certainly jeopardize the chances of the U.S. to remain the powerful and competitive country that it is now. For this reason, among others, minority students must experience success in school and in life.

A major challenge to improving the quality of education for all students, regardless of their economic level or race, is the development and distribution of sensitive, knowledgeable, and qualified teachers among the various schools (urban and rural) that serve poor and minority students. But the teachers who are assigned to teach in

8

schools where minority students are in attendance often are the ones least prepared to provide them with adequate instruction. Also, it has been recently reported that many minority teachers will leave teaching within five years.

Who, then, will teach the urban or rural poor, whether they are black, brown, Asian, or native American? It is of paramount importance that caring and sensitive non-minority teachers be assigned to classrooms where minority students attend in large numbers.

------

1. Christine E. Sleeter and Carl A. Grant, "Success for All Students," *Phi Delta Kappan* 68 (December 1986): 298.

2. Ibid., p. 297.

3. William Snider, "Hispanic Students Require Income to Remain in School," *Education Week*, September 21, 1988, p. 17.

Teachers and administrators may request copies of the report of the Hispanic Policy Development Project by writing to:

Hispanic Information Center
Suite 310
1001 Connecticut Avenue, N.W.
Washington, D.C. 20036
Request copes of "To Late to Patch."

A hundred years from now it will not matter what my bank account was, the sort of house I lived in, or the kind of car I drove. But, the world may be different because I was important in the life of a child.

Author unknown,
reprinted in "Progressive Farmer"

Chapter 3
Facilitating Learning and Achievement

> An instructor affects eternity; he can never tell
> where his influence ends.
>> Henry B. Adams

Schools exist to facilitate student learning and achievement. They also nurture and stimulate receptive minds to acquire knowledge and skills. Because education for minority students generally must be more structured than that provided to non-minority students, teachers must be inclined to ask themselves four key questions:

"What is it that helps students to learn?"

"What is it that teachers can do to aid their students in learning?"

"What teacher qualities, personal and professional, do I possess that help or hinder student learning?"

"What skills must teachers possess if they are to facilitate learning and achievement for minority students?"

There are five aspects of teaching that facilitate learning and achievement for minority students. They are: 1) teacher interest in the area of instruction, 2) role modeling by the instructor, 3) constructive and regular student evaluation, 4) high teacher expectations, and 5) use of questioning skills to actively involve students in the learning process.

Instructor Interest

The teacher's interest in instructing shows in many ways. Students are very perceptive and recognize teachers who do not wish to be

11

in a particular classroom or who are unsure of how or what to teach. Teachers who are interested in their classes must show their concern for teaching on a verbal level, on a nonverbal level, and on the strength of their classroom organization and management skills.

On a verbal level, the teacher's interest in instructing is evidenced by the facility with which materials are presented. In other words, the teacher must be prepared to tailor the lesson to the students' level of understanding. To be most effective, the teacher should project a professional image. Developing the ability to communicate extemporaneously with students is also of great importance, because students often will distract the teacher from the prepared lesson plans. The teacher will likely feel uneasy if he or she is not used to the unstructured and demanding environment alluded to here. This is natural and can only be overcome with practice. In the meantime, remember the "fake it till you feel it" axiom.

The teacher knows that a variety of techniques must be used to facilitate instruction with minority students. He or she is constantly searching for useful teaching methods that fit specific purposes and situations. In lending balance to the teaching techniques, the teacher will systematically plan and organize subject matter by gradient in a logical sequential order. The thrust of instruction, to a large degree, must be geared to the needs of the underprepared student.

Role Modeling

A key to student learning is role modeling. This may be more difficult than it sounds. For example, if a teacher professes "patience" to students, then that teacher should model patience while students question facts, confront frustration, attain knowledge, or display idiosyncrasies common to their level of maturity and judgment. If a teacher wants students to think, then he or she should model the ability to analyze, to think in a logical manner, and to process ideas, all of which require a great deal of patience and self-confidence. As stated by Johanna K. Lemlech in *Handbook for Successful Urban Teaching*,

> Modeling is to provide students with an example (a mirror) of appropriate behavior.[1]

Role models are sorely needed in classrooms where minority students are in attendance. Many of these students need teachers who can act out familiar life patterns for them. Teachers must be aware of this and must consistently display positive and mature behavior for their students to emulate. Emulation is vitally important to minority students. Teachers who model behaviors that affect the lives of minority students have a chance to succeed in ways that other teachers may not be privileged to enjoy.

Personal appearance is very important to minority students. Teachers should give strict attention to their appearance and attire. Students do not expect teachers to wear the most expensive clothes, but they do appreciate their being fashionable. Being well-groomed is an asset to teachers who work with minority students.

If teachers assign an abundance of library work, then they also should spend time in the library. Teachers who require research of students should find time to browse through the library themselves. There must be an open commitment to continuous learning. "To teach is to learn" should be stated and then demonstrated.

A sound oral vocabulary is an asset in any classroom. But in minority-dominated classrooms, it is an absolutely essential. It may be tempting, and sometimes necessary, to communicate using colloquialisms or the slang terms and idioms that some students use. However, the teacher's role is to entice students to express themselves in correct English. In order to do this, the teacher will have to motivate students to want to speak correctly by demonstrating how use of proper English will help students in reaching their goals. Moreover, teachers should be sensitive to the fact that students often need assistance in understanding and decoding the language. Often an apparent refusal to speak standard English is really a student's defensiveness about never having properly learned the language.

Student Evaluation

The teacher's active involvement in using effective and humane techniques of student evaluation is necessary for the facilitation of student learning. This process requires much planning, coordination, and an abundance of energy. This phase of teaching can be very demanding.

The teacher must keep in mind that materials taught may frequently be perceived by students as complicated or difficult, and that students can not be forced to learn unwillingly. A human approach to dealing with this kind of situation would be to adopt a teaching/evaluation format called Competency-Based Instruction (CBI).[2] The principle that underlies CBI is the criterion-reference teaching and evaluation system. This system holds the students accountable for meeting the objectives of the course, while the time for completing the objectives remains relative.

Students sometimes need to be baited in order to whet their appetite for learning. One teacher known for his baiting technique would say to his classes at the beginning of each semester: "Students, on this day I am assigning each of you a letter grade of A. This is my way of saying that each of you will start out with the highest possible grade. However, it is up to you to maintain the A average. You may be assured of keeping it by 1) attending class on a regular basis, 2) participating in class discussions, 3) completing all assignments asked of you, and 4) achieving a ninety percent criterion score on the final examination." It may not be gratifying to know that the grades in this teacher's classes usually run from A through F. However, he gave the students a chance to start out with a grade of A and a chance to keep the grade if they met his criteria.

The intent of this "baiting" is to allow students to see that their receiving an A is totally within the realm of possibility; they just have to demonstrate in good faith that they are willing to work for the reward that is offered.

Some interpersonal skills that teachers may use in facilitating learning with minority students include:

1. Accepting students' ideas and feelings. Students have the right of ownership relative to their ideas and feelings.
2. Knowing your students' names. Avoid getting the attention of students with "you," "Hey you, in the blue dress," a pointed finger, and so forth.
3. Believing that every child is a winner. Everyone is good at something; seek that something in students.
4. Including your students in the lesson planning process.
5. Maintaining an "integrated" personality. Be open and sensitive to the needs of students. Also, show a concern for personal growth and development.

Teacher Expectations

Teacher expectations determine to a considerable extent how much students will learn. "Believe in me!" is a line from a popular song that rings true in teaching. Its message is about someone wanting to be trusted, and who is capable of doing what is expected of him.

Too often teachers stymie student learning by holding low expectations of their capabilities. The Rosenthal and Jacobson studies[3] and research conducted by Robert D. Strom[4] arrive at empirically based conclusions that student learning generally parallels teacher expectations. This means that the teacher's high expectations are essential to promoting learning.

It is incumbent on teachers to expect their students to perform to the maximum of their potential. This expectation may not be borne out in the performance of all the students under a teacher's supervision, but a psychological boost provided by the teacher will encourage students in their quest for excellence.

When teachers believe their students are capable of learning and performing, this communicates a powerful message to them. The message contains hope, assurance, positive intentions, and most of all the belief that the students have worth. Teacher expectations affect student learning either positively or negatively.

Questioning Skills

Socrates, the Greek philosopher, was a highly regarded teacher. His competence was based on his effective use of questioning skills. Socrates' teaching approach was based on asking students a myriad of questions and probing their minds on several levels for answers.

Teachers should have a variety of questioning techniques at their disposal. They should make asking questions the heart of their teaching approach. According to research conducted by Lemlech:

> Questioning skills include classification tactics, refocusing tactics, redirecting, and the use of silence as a teaching technique.[5]

With the exercise of good questioning skills, teachers can stimulate most students, prompting them to become active participants in the discussion at hand. Additionally, cognitive and affective learning may be greatly enhanced through the process of questioning that invites creative and independent thinking. Minority students can be quite verbal outside the classroom; they need to develop verbal prowess through question-and-answer sessions in the classroom as well.

Why is the questioning phase of teaching important? Teaching efforts should run from the lowest to the highest levels of Bloom's taxonomic levels of instruction.[6] Most teaching is clustered around the knowledge and comprehension levels of learning. The use of questioning, including student interaction, will increase student understanding and achievement at other levels of instruction.

The use of higher-order questions must be included in the teacher's repertoire when questioning tactics are employed. As cited in Lemlech's research, the teacher is able to add variety and understanding to the teaching process through the use of effective questioning skills.

Summary

For the most part, effective teaching results in student learning. At times, though, effective teaching may not result in accomplishment.

To facilitate student learning, teachers must be familiar with more than the traditional methods that promote (or impede) the social, personal, psychological, and intellectual growth of students. The facilitation of student growth toward desired ends demands that new skills be employed to accommodate unique and varied student needs.

---

1. Johanna K. Lemlech, *Handbook for Successful Urban Teaching* (San Francisco: Harper & Row, 1977), pp. 87-89.

2. In Competency Based Instruction, students achieve criterion scores based on specified competencies.

3. Robert Rosenthal and Lenore Jacobson, *Pygmalion in the Classroom* (New York: Holt, Rinehard and Winston, 1968).

4. Robert D. Strom, "The School Dropout and the Family," *School and Society* 92 (April 1964): 191-92.

5. Lemlech, op. cit., pp. 91-93.

6. Benjamin S. Bloom, ed., *Taxonomy of Educational Objectives, The Classification of Educational Goals — Handbook I: Cognitive Domain* (New York: David McKay, 1956).

Without good schools,
none of our problems can be solved.

People who cannot communicate are powerless.

People who know nothing of their past
are culturally impoverished.

People who cannot see beyond
the confines of their own lives
are ill-equipped to face the future.

It is in the public school that this nation
has chosen to pursue enlightened ends
for all its people.

And this is where the battle for the future of America
will be won or lost.

> *High School,* Ernest L. Boyer
> Carnegie Foundation for the
> Advancement of Teaching, 1983.

Chapter 4
Educators Developing Cultural Sensitivity

Everybody is ignorant, only on different subjects.
Will Rogers

Educators practice in a profession where they are expected to have a thorough preparation in teacher education skills and methodologies, to be intimately familiar with the subject matter they teach, to subscribe to the ethics of the profession of education, and to be aware of cultural practices and ideologies, however varied they may be. A vast amount of information is embodied in these topics, making it difficult for teachers to master each of them.

Schools reflect the values of the larger society in which they exist and sometimes are considered microcosms of that society. As the demographic makeup of our country changes, it becomes increasingly vital that we be aware of cultural influences that may hinder or facilitate our effectiveness in teaching students, regardless of their social, cultural, ethnic, religious, or racial background. Given the growing diversity of our country, this is becoming a very complex task. We, as educators, are some of the most learned scholars in society. Yet our relative success in teaching may be diluted if we are ineffective in teaching a certain segment of students such as minority students.

Educators must be concerned with the quality of education that minority students are receiving and, equally as important, with their own need to develop sensitivity to different cultures. If this can not be accomplished through teacher training programs, teachers must assume the task of developing adequate cultural sensitivity on their own.

Teachers and school administrative personnel are generally motivated to participate in activities geared toward professional growth and development. But if they do not have this kind of motivation, an article that appeared recently in *Education Week* may be helpful:

> California has reached an historic turning point: This year, a majority of its public school students are members of minority groups. Figures released by the [California] State Department of Education show that Hispanics, Blacks, Asians, and other minorities make up an estimated 50.8 percent of the 4.6 million students in California schools this year. Whites remain the largest ethnic group, constituting 49.2 percent of students. Hispanic students are next at 30.7 percent; followed by Blacks at 9.0 percent; Asians, 7.6 percent; Filipinos at 2.2 percent; Native Americans, 0.8 percent; and Pacific Islanders, 0.5 percent.[1]

California is unique. However, it is not uncommon elsewhere to find communities where minority students make up 50 percent (or more) of the enrollment in public schools. With an ever-increasing number of minority-group children being born, we can expect many more American cities (and even smaller communities) to have sizable percentages of minority students enrolled in the schools.

Just before the above-mentioned article appeared, there was a status report in *School Board News* regarding minority students:

> In most of the nation's largest urban school districts, a majority of the students are members of minority groups. Among the states, Hawaii, Mississippi, and New Mexico have majority "minority" public school enrollments. . .[2]

Harold Hodgkinson[3] also has provided educators with demographic data on population shifts and trends in education in the 1990s and beyond that will make schools markedly different from those that educators have known. Educators and the education profession must, of necessity, come to grips with the multitude of socioeducational concerns that minority students present. Educators now must develop minority perspectives on educational matters.

The challenge of educating large numbers of minority students faces educators. But the greatest challenge now is for educators to develop new, specialized teaching skills. Educators need to be certain that minority students are provided the education they deserve and need. In this regard, educators must manage their shortcomings better than they have done in the past.

Colleges and universities must play a role in promoting respect for cultural sensitivity and the reduction of cultural ignorance. Their direction is found in the AACTE Board of Directors statement, "No One Model American," that was issued in 1972. An excerpt of the statement reads:

> Colleges and universities engaged in training teachers have a central role in the positive development of our culturally pluralistic society. If cultural pluralism is to become an integral part of the educational process, teachers and personnel must be prepared in an environment where the commitment to multicultural education is evident. . . . Multicultural education programs for teachers are more than special courses or special learning experiences grafted onto the standard program. The commitment to cultural pluralism must permeate all areas of the educational experience provided for prospective teachers.[4]

One of the most enduring aspects of teaching is the professional growth and development that must take place if we are to carry out fully our professional responsibilities. No matter what kind of year we experienced last year or the year before, the year we are *in* is destined to be better.

The reason for this degree of optimism, of course, is the challenge that teaching brings. Educators know that when the "tough get going, the going gets tough." And when coping with shortcomings that may exist in our professional skills, we can take initiatives to manage them. A large percentage of educators work with students from unfamiliar cultures and thus must develop better cultural sensitivity.

Corrective action to reduce cultural ignorance in educators is sorely needed. A host of socioeducational problems facing school personnel may be attributed to this. Many minority students and their teachers have become indifferent to the cultural differences separating them because they lack familiarity with each others' cultural milieu.

According to Frank Besag,[5] many problems facing schools will continue to be unresolved, not because the problems are insolvable, but because they are being viewed from the perspective of the supposed necessity that teachers enforce justifiable sets of cultural patterns (as they know them) on students. Because of such attitudes, effective and meaningful interaction between teachers and minority students may be hindered, and purposeful learning may not take place at the level that is desired.

Developing cultural sensitivity requires learning, as stated by Peters and Austin in *A Passion for Excellence*:

> To learn is to change; and to change can be both exhilarating and wrenching. As creatures of habit, we must approach learning with trepidation, not expecting those who learn to experience a smooth trajectory of triumphs, nor those who teach to effect unrelieved excitement about their subject. . . . It is true that what is most easily learned is usually hardest taught . . .[6]

Many teacher training programs must share in the blame for the cultural insensitivity that currently exists. The teachers of today's and tomorrow's schools must be prepared to function in settings in which they are responsible for students from a multiplicity of cultural backgrounds.[7] Unfortunately, many institutions devoted to teacher preparation are in monocultural settings and may not have programs designed to carry out this commitment.

Because some teacher training programs do not provide opportunities for multicultural education experiences (as are profiled in a case study by Fuller and Ahler on multicultural education and the training of teachers[8]), preservice and inservice teachers must take it upon themselves to seek out opportunities for cultural growth. One such initiative for professional growth is highlighted in a paper written by Lydia Young, an inservice teacher enrolled at a Texas university. The teacher visited a church attended by a predominantly Black congregation. A synopsis of the paper follows:

My Visit to a Black Church

I attended Greater Faith Methodist Church last summer. Not having attended a Black church since my childhood days, my expectations and anxieties towards the visit were varied. One always wonders what reception one will receive when going into a place where you know you will be in the minority. So it was with the dualistic feeling of anticipation and hesitation that I proceeded.

While I was walking from the parking lot to the door of the church, some people turned to look; some seemed pleased to have me come, and others tried to hide their obvious interest.

At the door, the usher, smiling warmly, welcomed me to the church. I breathed a silent sigh of relief and thought — so far, so good. As I proceeded into the church, a few people said hello with a warmth that put me at ease. A few seemed not to notice my presence, but most watched as I took my seat. A young couple came and sat next to me; again, I felt that my being there was not offensive.

The church was nice inside, but I was surprised to find metal folding chairs and a linoleum floor. The altar was simplistic, much on the style of many churches I have been in.

The service was conducted very much like the services of the Episcopal church (my affiliation) and was much more formal and subdued than I had expected. Even the singing was hushed. White Southern Baptists sing with more "gusto" than I found in this church. It seemed too quiet, as though the congregation had rather not be singing. We sang two of my favorite hymns, "Holy, Holy, Holy" and "Let Us Break Bread Together." I wanted so much for the walls to ring with the joy and meaning in them, but we sang quietly on.

After the service, some of the members told me they were glad I had come, that they hoped I had enjoyed the service, and invited me to come again. The Reverend Charles Haskins extended the same welcome to me.

The only real difference I noted was in the make-up of the congregation. There were few teenagers and few men. There were several young couples, but most attending were women and children. The ushers for the communion were four teenagers, two girls and two boys. The duplicating machine was broken (as the Reverend Haskins said, "Due to the Devil's work!") so there was no bulletin this Sunday.

The people were proud of their church and were warm and friendly to me.

As I think about it, it seems that people are too afraid to reach out to know others, particularly those of a different ethnic group. But with all the prejudices, hostilities, and stereotyping that exist today, this experience has reinforced my belief that someone has to make the first step, unsure as it may seem, towards stepping over these barriers. I believe this experience will help me in taking more first steps towards other people. I am sure that not all future experiences will be like the one I had, but there is the knowledge that there are common meeting grounds; that finding them is the challenge and my small way of meeting people and accepting them.

When one expects to be met with bias, one will probably find it. I went to the Black church a little anxious over my reception and found warmth and hospitality. This positive experience has added to my life perspectives about people of another race and their orientation to a common experience, religion in this case, that people share.

In some ways, this experience provided me with personal and professional development I wish I had experienced while at the university preparing to become a teacher. Social interaction with culturally and racially different people is so important to one's growth in becoming a successful and competent teacher.

This kind of valuable experience cannot be gained in textbooks. To experience something firsthand is to be an intimate part of it.

The most important resource of the schools is their teachers. Perhaps the thing most needed for the care and nurturing of this great resource is a desire on the part of teachers to remain learners. Teachers must endeavor to grow. Social and educational situations demand that growth opportunities be engaged in actively.

If an adequate understanding of multicultural education principles is not provided in teacher preparation programs, educators must go out and manage their understanding of cultural matters. Toward these ends, educators can develop skills that have positive impact on the interpersonal dynamics that surface when they interact with minority students. There is much to be gained when teachers develop skills in teaching minority students; education then can be raised to optimal levels.

1. "In California: Nation's First Minority Majority," *Education Week*, September 21, 1988, p. 3.

2. "Districts Aggressively Recruit Minority Teachers," *School Board News*, September 14, 1988, p. 1.

3. Harold Hodgkinson, *All One System: Demographics of Education* (Washington, D.C.: Institute for Educational Leadership, 1985).

4. "No One Model American," a product of the Commission on Multicultural Education, was adopted officially in November 1972 by the AACTE Board of Directors as a guide for addressing the issue of multicultural education.

5. Frank Besag, "Cultural Ignorance," in *Encyclopedia of School Administration and Supervision*, edited by Richard A. Gorton *et al*. (Phoenix: Oryx Press, 1988), p. 252.

6. Tom Peters and Nancy Austin, *A Passion for Excellence*. (New York: Random House, 1985), p. 252.

7. Mary Lou Fuller and Janet Ahler, "Multicultural Education and the Monocultural Student: A Case Study," in *Action in Teacher Education* 9, no. 3 (Fall 1987): 33. This is a highly recommended case study for directors of teacher education programs.

8. Ibid, pp. 33-41.

WORDS OF WISDOM

Risk . . .

To laugh is to risk being the fool.

To weep is to risk appearing sentimental.

To reach out for another is to risk involvement.

To expose feelings is to risk exposing your true self.

To place your ideas, your dreams, before a group is to risk their loss.

To love is to risk not being loved in return.

To live is to risk dying.

To hope is to risk despair.

To try is to risk failure.

But risks must be taken, because the greatest hazard in life is to risk nothing.

The person who risks nothing has nothing, and is nothing.

They may avoid suffering and sorrow, but they cannot LEARN . . . FEEL . . . CHANGE . . . GROW . . . LOVE . . . OR LIVE

Chained by their attitudes, they are slaves, for they have forfeited their freedom.

Only a person who risks is free.

Author Unknown

Chapter 5
Teaching the Exceptional Student

Exceptional students are those designated as having some physical or mental characteristics that make it necessary for teachers to think about them in special ways. The designation of "exceptional" includes the exceptionally bright or exceptionally dull student, the student with severe vision or hearing defects, the crippled student, or the student with cerebral palsy.

An exceptional student, like any other, has dignity, worth, emotions, and feelings. A teacher should view the handicapped student as having as much learning potential as any other student. This is essential in today's schools, where federal and state statutes mandate that handicapped children be provided equal educational opportunity.

Exceptional children may have emotional and mental health needs that must be nurtured in special ways. A cardinal principle for teachers working with exceptional students, especially if they are minority students, is to help them realize their maximal potential within whatever limitations they may have.

It is extremely important that teachers refrain from making exceptions for the exceptional student. This may be difficult, but it is essential in order for the educational program to be carried out for the benefit of the student. Many factors go into the developmental needs of the exceptional student.

Concerning exceptional students, schools generally best look after the educational needs of the academically dull student because their needs are far greater than the needs of those in the regular school program or programs for the gifted.

With regard to the gifted, the teacher has a greater responsibility to these students, for they can easily become bored with school life and fail to develop their strong intellectual potential. Exceptional students classified as "gifted" may easily become behavioral problems if their needs are not targeted and met.

It is advantageous to the teacher to have had courses in special education or in the principles of mainstreaming. A number of special policies and practices are recommended in teaching special students, so it is wise to learn how the experts advise that exceptional students be taught. It is a rarity for a classroom not to have students in it who will be separated out for programs that are designed to meet their special needs.

Historically, minority students have often been tracked into programs that are not challenging or academically fitting to bring out their best talents. Numerous court cases have been filed on behalf of minority students and their right to a quality education.

Tracking is *not* the way to carry out the best procedures in working with the academically dull student; however, some school districts still carry out some semblance of tracking under the guise of best providing for the needs of students. But if one were to look at the composition of classes that are tracked, it would be obvious that the majority of the students — if not all — are minority students. And therein lies a tragedy in the way education is carried out with regard to the exceptional student.

It is incumbent on teachers to develop strategies and techniques in working with students who are classified as exceptional. In some way, everyone is exceptional; and in this regard, we have to assess means and strategies for providing delivery systems that will best improve learning for all students. Race is *not* a determiner in providing for students' needs.

In planning programs for the exceptional student, one should read the provisions of Public Law 94-142 carefully. This law is the basis for many of the programs now mandated for schools on behalf of exceptional students. In addition to this statute, state departments of education also provide special program funding for gifted and talented students. School districts across the country have special offices specifically for the handicapped and special student. It also is recommended that teachers talk to administrators and persons designated to handle the special programs about ways to further the learning potential of students classified as exceptional.

To conquer the fear of failing
you need only remain open
and willing to succeed.

Rod McKuen

Chapter 6
Exit Examinations Are Not the Problem

Change is vital. Change is inevitable. Yet change can be very painful, especially if a student is told that he or she will not receive a high school diploma but instead a certificate of attendance. This will soon happen in many states because of legislation that requires students to complete an exit examination before receiving a high school diploma.

Who will eventually be a high school graduate? Who will instead receive the certificate of attendance? These questions will be answered at the close of the 1989-90 academic year when both the diploma and the certificate of attendance are awarded to South Carolina high school seniors. The state of South Carolina passed legislation to improve the image of high school graduates in that state. The legislation is certainly rigorous; however, it was introduced with adequate warning. The students who graduate with South Carolina high school diplomas in 1989 were high school freshmen when the legislation was finally adopted. They will be the first class to submit to the mandate requiring them to pass an examination in the basic skills.

Students intending to graduate from high school during the 1989-90 school year must first pass the South Carolina Exit Examination. Their failure to pass the examination obligates them to enroll in a remedial program. Students who do not pass the examination in the tenth grade must retake it in the eleventh grade and may take it twice in the twelfth grade, thereby providing them with four chances to pass.

Evidence suggests that some students need to be pressured into performing in classroom activities and on external achievement assessments. A high school diploma should indicate more than the fact that a student has attended school for a requisite number of years.

31

It is incumbent on schools to be able to attest to the fact that their students possess minimal skills prior to high school graduation.

There is a fear in some quarters that the exit examination will affect a large number of minority students. The fear is justifiable: a fairly high percentage of minority students will probably fail the examination during its initial run. But another reality will also be apparent: the exit examination is not the problem; it will, however, expose the problem.

Because minority students will likely be the ones to fail high school exit examinations (in South Carolina and in other states), teachers must take more than a casual interest in the well-being of their students with regard to their passing the examination.

There are three essential strategies teachers can use to assist students who need help in achieving passing scores on exit examinations:

1. Be certain that the course content that is on the examination is adequately taught. The curriculum from which course content is taught must parallel to a large degree items on the examination.
2. Provide practice opportunities for students to gain familiarity with the kinds of questions that are covered on the examination. These practice opportunities should be given on the same time basis as are the mock examinations used in practice sessions.
3. *Empower* students to take their destiny in their own hands. This means that students must be encouraged to believe they can pass any examination that comes before them.

Unlike the voluntary SAT and ACT, a passing score on the exit examination is required by state law to determine whether students are awarded a high school diploma or a certificate of attendance. It remains to be seen if a fairly large percentage of minority students are awarded the certificate of attendance as their exit visa after twelve years of school attendance. Teachers must have the resolve and capacity to see that students pass the examination.

What is really important in education is not that the child learns this and that, but that the mind is matured, that energy is aroused.

Sören Kierkegaard

Chapter 7
Beyond the Basic Skills

Equipping students with strong basic skills no longer will
ensure their success in the job market.
> Education Commission of the States, 1988

Many of the educational problems of minority students are rooted in educational practices that thwart student educational programs. As schools are currently constituted, they have little influence or impact on changing society in terms of its employment practices, racism (blatant or covert), civil rights practices, human relations, and other societally induced problems that minorities face.

Schools are microcosms of society; they reflect, for better or worse, the general conditions of society. In some ways, schools may aggravate and add to the existing inequalities and inequities of American society. The role of the school essentially is determined by the dominant philosophy of the society in which its people live and work. The structure and function of schools, whether in totalitarian societies or in democratic countries, must meet the expressed needs of the culture and its inherent ideologies.

It is suggested in some parts of the American society that minority students need strong measures of the basic skills — reading, writing, and mathematics — to succeed in life. To some extent, this is true; but the suggestion reveals flawed educational practice. Providing only a heavy dose of basic skills is of questionable benefit to millions of minority students who leave school each year.

The world that is dawning now is a world in which people will constantly be forced to make adjustments in their lives. Conditions

35

of life and modern lifestyles reflect the technological age that is already upon us. If minority students are to find a satisfactory niche in tomorrow's world, they will need much more than what basic skills provide.

Minority students, like all other students, must develop technological skills. They need the ability to process ideas and concepts of a technical nature. The school's curriculum must be revamped to include studies in futuristics and probabilities. The school curriculum in which students participate must not relegate them to the fringes of a quality education.

Students know the difference between learning a subject that has substance as opposed to going through worthless motions and jumping through hoops. Today's students *want* to learn. It is amazing how many inferior programs are offered to thousands of minority students each year. Except for the students who are fortunate and learn to "beat" the system at its own game, the average minority student goes through school enrolling in routine courses that are taught as though they were nothing more than basic skills.

Teachers must move beyond the basic skills with their students. Many teachers who teach nothing but the basic skills year after year discover that they tire of the repetitiveness, regardless of how much they profess to love their subject matter. To counter this, teachers need to integrate the basic skills with information that will help students adapt well to the future. This implies that teachers do more than teach mathematics, science, reading, and writing as single subjects. The prospects for student success and teacher satisfaction using this organizational format may appear limitless and positive. But, in the main, it is necessary to move beyond the basic skills.

All things are possible once enough human beings realize that the whole of the human future is at stake.

Author Unknown

Chapter 8
Child Abuse: A School and Societal Problem

According to Lois Distad, educators assume that the academic failures of elementary school children are usually caused by skill deficits, developmental delays, learning disabilities, or poor teaching. They debate the detrimental effects of harsh economics or emotional upheaval on children's capacity for school learning. The message that many of these children express through their learning problems — the message that their teachers too often miss — is the misery of child abuse.[1]

Teachers in classrooms where minority students are in attendance will likely come into contact with those who are abused by parents, guardians, or other persons who frequent their residences. When child abuse situations do occur, teachers must be able to identify abused students and make life and school conditions better for them, however temporarily. Toward these ends, teachers must:

1. Recognize the overt symptoms of child abuse.
2. Report suspicions of child abuse to the principal or other authorities who may be able to provide guidance and direction.
3. Talk to the student. Establish a level of rapport that will encourage the student to inform school authorities of abuse that may have occurred or is occurring.
4. Use teaching strategies and methodologies that raise the self-esteem of the student.
5. Refer the student to the guidance counselor or other school specialists who are designated to work with abused students.

Child abuse is shockingly prevalent in today's society. Child abuse is no respecter of ethnic, racial, religious, or socioeconomic origin or position. Child abusers care little about the emotional, psychological, and physical abuse of their victims.

Expressions over the horrors of child abuse will continue to be in the news. But expressions of horror will not reduce the amount of child abuse without concerted and corrective action taken by key professionals — namely teachers. Placing blame on the child abuser and his or her problems will not solve the problem either; teachers helping students to help themselves is an important part of the solution.

Teachers also must assist students in understanding that they are human beings with feelings and emotions and that others may not harm their bodies or transgress upon their feelings and emotions. Unlike bodily harm, emotional and psychological abuse may be hard to detect. Students must be taught through precept and model behavior by teachers that all persons — regardless of their age — have worth and dignity that must be protected and, if need be, defended.

If students are taught to feel good about themselves, then some of their reticence at communicating when questioned about child abuse may be eliminated. When this happens, school personnel may begin to witness a moderate reduction in the number of child abuse cases that are observed.

Minority students are highly vulnerable to child abuse. Because of the prevailing attitudes of court systems, and the fact that the child abuser, too, is usually a minority, the prosecution of offenders may be less than effective. It might be an easier task for teachers to work systematically with abused students and the concerned guardian than it is to improve conditions in the judicial system.

At school, another kind of child abuse occurs. Some minority students, like students of other ethnic or racial backgrounds, are often the victims of "teacher talk" in the office lounge. There, some of the most bitter attacks against students take place. These attacks may not be directly physical, social, or emotional, but the indirect damage is just as damaging to the student. Students' reputations can be tarnished or destroyed, although teachers may not have intended it.

Teachers can assist minority students in the area of child abuse at two levels: 1) help them live with the trauma that will certainly enter their lives because of conditions at home and elsewhere; and 2) make the school and classroom secure places for them so that these two areas are hospitable, palatable, and free from additional abuse.

---

1. Lois Distad, "A Personal Legacy," *Phi Delta Kappan* 68 (June 1987): 733-45.

MY TEACHER

From the moment we met in class,
*   I knew you were to be different.*
There was something about you
*   that set me at ease.*

When I'm in your class and laboratory,
*   I'm free to feel important; free to say and do.*
Frankly, I feel lucky this year
*   to have found a caring teacher like you.*

Like me, you speak Spanish,
*   and I believe you understand me.*
Since elementary school,
*   no one has touched me like you.*

So, from the moment we met,
*   I knew you were going to be in my corner.*
Teacher, I like you; I need you.
*   May this be a very good year for both of us.*

Carlos Martinez
10th-Grade Biology

Chapter 9
Communicating Through Other Languages and Dialects

To teach minority students successfully, teachers must acquire communication skills in the languages the students know best. Where applicable, familiarity with Spanish, ghettoese, Vietnamese, pidgin English, Gullah, Tex-Mex, and native American dialects can be helpful to academic progress in the classroom. A wide variety of languages and unusual speech patterns often are displayed in classrooms where minority students are in attendance.

Why is a familiarity with other languages and dialects important? Language and dialect are vital to communication between people and are necessary tools for encouraging a cultural exchange between teachers and students. Most importantly, common language usage permits teachers and students to have a shared base from which to understand each other.

This kind of familiarity can bring students and teachers together. This bridge serves as a link or common denominator for facilitating the kind of understanding necessary to promoting greater student achievement and learning gains.

Teachers' familiarity with the native languages of students allows students to see that their teachers appreciate languages and dialects that are found in their home and community. It also allows teachers to understand and use different means to communicate with students.

The monolingual teacher is at a considerable disadvantage in a classroom with minority students. This teacher's limited repertoire of language skills may, in some instances, hinder the achievement and learning that might be possible if he were able to communicate in other languages and dialects.

It is never too late to correct this shortcoming. First, teachers must recognize that the knowledge and understanding of different languages and dialects is a genuine asset in the classroom. If a teacher's knowledge base is not yet developed in this area, it must be developed at all costs. This may be accomplished in several ways. Three are recommended:

1. Enroll in special courses at a college or university. In addition to the language course of specialization, enroll in companion cultural and/or anthropological courses. This may take time and money, but the effort will result in added benefits for students because of one's enhancement of language skills and their appropriate usage.

2. Purchase special auditory language materials. For instance, the Berlitz program is readily available in various methods and languages. This program allows the teacher to go at a pace that is adapted to his own needs. In addition to the convenience of this language program, it also provides immediate feedback without teacher monitoring or the burden of class assignments. The outcome is the same – proficiency in the acquisition of one or more language skills.

3. Study languages with native speakers or families in the community in which one teaches. This is preferable to the first two recommendations; however, this depends on the willingness of a family to engage in studious inquiry while at the same time fostering a social relationship with the teacher. Toward this end, a teacher should strive to develop a rapport with persons who are amenable to assisting him in developing proficiency in the use of second- or third-language skills.

Whether it is a foreign language or a dialect that is particular to a certain region of the U.S., teachers who work with minority students must expect to hear languages or dialects specific to those students. It is therefore incumbent on persons who teach in these classrooms not only to be prepared to teach subject matter through content, process, and evaluation skills, but also to teach these skills through the language or dialect that students are most familiar with and can understand.

Teachers must monitor student language usage very closely. Speaking ghettoese, Spanish, Gullah, or any of the other common dialects may hinder the development of the students' proficient use of standard English. Non-standard English, dialects, and other speech patterns may be useful to the student in the home, on the playground, and in the community; but with standardized examinations, employment applications, and other situations where standard English is essential, these speech patterns and dialects will not serve the students in good stead.

For professional educators to succeed in classrooms where minority students are in attendance, they must be familiar with and demonstrate an understanding of different languages and speech patterns. Most importantly, they must use them as a means to help students develop sufficient means of standard communication that will serve them well in school and throughout life.

Children have never been good at listening to their elders, but they have never failed to imitate them.

James Baldwin

Chapter 10
Global and Multicultural
Understanding Skills

As a general rule, teachers teach more
by what they are than by what they say.
Anonymous

Minority students who enter kindergarten in 1989 will graduate from high school during the twenty-first century. In many ways, the world in which they live will be vastly different from the one their parents and grandparents knew in the twentieth century. They will certainly know about lasers, superconductivity research, space explorations, the increasing interdependence of nations, and family situations that are governed by different mores of acceptance.

Minority youth, like all other youth of the future, also must understand that economic, political, and cultural developments in the United States and elsewhere will no longer occur within distinct state and national boundaries. Globalization of the marketplace will usher in a need for understanding and respecting other nations and peoples. The strength of a democratic world will be demonstrated through the utilization of expertise from various groups and organizations in working toward shared goals for the betterment of humanity and world peace.

One of the school's major responsibilities in preparing youth for future roles is to teach them to adapt to the many groups in which they will find themselves. In the past, this has meant preparing them for membership in local, regional, and national communities. But this is no longer a viable option because they will have to adapt to living in a global society. Toward these ends, they will have to develop knowledge, skills, and attitudes that will prepare them to adapt to whatever situations in which they find themselves.

Take, for example, the Olympics that took place in Seoul in 1988. On this occasion, millions of people around the globe experienced a vicarious relationship with the Olympics. South Korea was on display; and personal and political ideologies of athletes from various countries were inspected, along with their cultural and value orientations.

Several important questions come to mind, such as how teachers can help prepare students for a world where minorities are the majority? What skills, attitudes, and values are important to them for use in their daily lives? What resources will these students need to develop their perceptual awareness of life from a global standpoint? What does it mean to promote global and multicultural understanding skills?

First, teachers themselves must promote and exemplify behavior and skills of global and multicultural understanding. This means that students have to be in classroom environments where cultural, ethnic, religious, racial, and other differences are respected. As James Banks says, "multicultural understanding should enable students to identify, respect, and suspend judgment concerning the characteristics of a cultural group different from their own."[1] As can be witnessed by conflicts at home and abroad, this is a difficult task to carry out.

In this world of approximately 5 billion inhabitants, most of us are members of an ethnic minority. Minority students must now begin to shift their orientation, since they will eventually outnumber Caucasians. They must develop perspectives about life that will permit them to co-exist with all people. Life in the twenty-first century should not be a time to "get back" at certain groups for transgressions that they or their ancestors may have perpetrated. Nor must students now (or then) feel that they must act out their new-found majority status in inappropriate ways.

What can the schools do to promote positive attitudes and understanding with regard to skills in global and multicultural understanding for all? In sharing his views on the subject, Theodore Kaltsounis writes that students should:

> recognize and perceive the world as an interdependent human community made up of cultures which have more similarities than differences;

48

recognize the inevitability and benefits of diversity among people and cultures;

recognize the common problems facing the world community;

recognize the realities of world living, including conflict and need for peace;

recognize the constantly changing conditions and status of the world as well as certain fundamental values;

recognize individual self-worth; and

recognize that each individual's perception of the world is his own, shaped by his experiences and not necessarily shared by others.[2]

Life in the twenty-first century is going to be different for everyone. One has only to read the newspapers and watch television to see this happening.

The students of today are in preparation for the extension of their lives into the next century. It is of paramount importance that teachers teach and promote global and multicultural understanding skills for students, especially minority students, who will be a majority group in numbers in many communities — and possibly in other ways, too — by the time the twenty-first century rolls around. We cannot afford to do less.

---

1. James A. Banks, *Teaching Strategies for Ethnic Studies,* 2nd ed. (Boston: Allyn and Bacon, 1979), p. 23.

2. Theodore Kaltsounis, *Teaching Social Studies in the Elementary School* (Englewood Cliffs, N.J.: Prentice-Hall, 1987), p. 301.

Don't say, "I can't."
Say "I choose not to."

Russian Proverb

Chapter 11
Developing Communication and Rapport with Parents of Minority Students

If we are to teach minority students,
We first must reach the parent.
                                        Howard D. Hill

As an education professional, you must establish communication and rapport with the parents of minority students. One way to accomplish this is to invite the parents of minority students to school. A letter may be sent inviting them to have lunch, to visit their children's classroom, to meet the principal, or to witness a special activity.

Invitations should be written on personal stationery. Plan such visits for times when you are able to meet the parents (or guardians) as they arrive at the school. If at all possible, notify the children that their parents are on the premises.

As you consider this recommendation, remember that this is an important opportunity for you to reach out to a segment of the parents of students you may not know. For many minority students, this kind of courtesy is seldom extended to their parents.

This is also a chance for you to gain support, build confidence, and promote increased social, personal, and academic gains for students who often feel alienated from school. Express your reasons to the parents for inviting them to the school. As a teacher, you want them to know that their children are capable of doing well in school.

From this point on, explain to them why you feel that now is a very good time for their children to be attending school. Let the parents know that you have total confidence in their children's ability to achieve in school and later in life. What you desire from them at this time is their cooperation and support in helping you to promote the attainment of those goals for their children.

Because it is conducted on a school day, the visit will be relatively short; but you will be establishing communication and rapport with the parents. Do not fear extending the invitation to them. Commit yourself early in the school year to this activity and go slowly in meeting parents, especially parents whom you have not met previously and those you will not get to meet and visit with under more natural circumstances.

At the close of the day, write a note to the parents, thanking them for visiting with you and other school personnel. As you might imagine, as soon as the parents get home, they will immediately be telling their friends and neighbors what happened to them at school this day. But that's what you expected, right?

Minority parents generally:

- want their children to do well in school, even though a percentage of them may fail;
- desire that their children learn skills far beyond the basics;
- have hopes that the school will create opportunities for their children that they may have been denied; and
- can assist the school in carrying out many of its educational objectives.

There is ample evidence that parents are willing to do a great deal to assist the school in promoting programs; but school personnel *must* reach out to them and get to know them. It makes a lot of sense for you — the education professional — to take the initiative to establish communication and a good rapport with minority parents.

After a parental visit, it can be anticipated that some of the parents will wish to volunteer their time to the school. Should this occur, by all means explore ways to capitalize on it with the school administration. The presence of minority parents working with teachers and administrators in facilitating student achievement will send a strong message to the community: This school can establish communication and rapport with the parents of minority students.

In conclusion, if a school is to function effectively in the context of family and schooling, it is important that teachers and administrators become thoroughly knowledgeable and sensitive to the family and how it may promote quality education for the students who attend the school.

JUST A TEACHER

Today I was a nurse binding a hurt with the white
bandage of compassion,
A doctor healing a small, broken world,
A surgeon suturing a friendship together.

Today I was an alchemist seeking gold in base metals,
A scientist answering endless whys,
A philosopher pondering elusive truths.

Today, I was an entertainer, refreshing young minds
with laughter,
A fisherman dangling learning as a bait,
A pilot guiding youth away from ignorance.

Today, I was a general campaigning against
intolerance,
A lawyer speaking out for brotherhood,
A juror weighing right and wrong.

Today, I was a philanthropist sharing the might of the
past,
A mother wholly giving love,
A humble follower of truth.

Mine are such varied occupations,
I am "just a teacher."

Author Unknown

Chapter 12
Home Visitations for Teachers

*There is one thing stronger than all the armies of the world;
and that is an idea whose time has come.*

Victor Hugo

In recent years, teachers have become keenly aware that schools are not necessarily the most significant influences in the lives of students, especially minority students. Thus, the power of schools to mold and shape students is not as strong as once was believed. Parents, schools, social agencies, police departments, churches, and the community also contribute to the educational progress of today's students.

Surprisingly little debate about the proper role and responsibilities of parents has surfaced in the current wave of concern over the plight of public education.[1] Does this mean that parents are no longer interested in the total education of their children? Have parents decided that teachers and schools know best what to do about educating their children, and so are now willing to yield great *in loco parentis* powers to the teachers? Are there currently conflicts between teachers and parents for which a cooling-off period is needed?

From the community viewpoint, the teacher is the most important person in the school system. Parents expect a great deal from the teachers of their children. In the elementary years, the teacher is responsible for teaching the basic skills — reading, writing, and arithmetic — and for providing formal instruction in other subjects. Parents expect their children to be successful in school and, when they are not, tend to blame the teacher and the school. The school, in many homes, is a prime topic of conversation and a factor in a number of family decisions.[2]

Because an unfavorable home environment may influence a student's attitude toward school, there is a great need to help minority students become successful in school. Improved communication between the home and school is imperative if this is to be accomplished.

Not too many years ago, home visitation was an important part of the teacher's job. Today, however, when home visitation is mentioned, teachers and administrators often react negatively. Some dislike having to plan visits to the homes of students. In certain instances, there even may be resistance to the idea by parents. This may contribute to the widening gap between schools' and parents' needs.

Teachers of minority students should make home visits. There may be risks involved, but the risks can be minimized with a balance of preparation and caution. By visiting students' homes, teachers may be able to discover the reasons for students' poor performance in school. Or they may be pleasantly surprised to meet parents who are supportive of their children, and may see how this contributes to their classroom and out-of-class behavior.

Kindergarten and elementary school teachers should visit most, if not all, of the students' homes each year. Unless these teachers change grade levels, they will not have the opportunity of teaching the same students on different occasions.

This is not necessarily the case for junior and senior high school students. While kindergarten and elementary school teachers teach 18 to 30 students in self-contained classrooms, junior and senior high school teachers may have as many as 75 to 150 students per day. In many cases junior high and high school teachers teach the same student on more than one occasion.

It should not be assumed that teachers must visit the homes of *all* their students each year. But teachers must make an attempt to visit as many homes as possible. They must visit homes of successful as well as less successful students.

Why Home Visitation?

Henderson has cited studies published by the National Committee for Citizens in Education that show how parents and teachers working together can sharpen students' academic and social skills. The studies suggest strongly that involving parents in education can make a critical difference. These studies focus on 1) improving the parent/child relationship, 2) introducing parent involvement in the school, and 3) building a partnership between home and school.[3] Home visitations must ultimately be viewed by teachers and parents as a chance to have the school and home function together on behalf of the student. This is what education is about.

Before a teacher attempts to visit the home of a student, preparation must be made for the visit. Parents should be contacted initially to see if they are amenable to having the teacher visit the home. If there is agreement to the visit, the student(s) in the home also must be informed of the visit. The teacher should consider the following questions:

1. Why do I wish to visit this home?
2. Is the student whose home I am to visit one of my better students or one who gives me problems at school?
3. If the student is of another race, how can I feel comfortable being in the home?
4. Is the community in which the home is located one that I feel comfortable visiting?
5. What do I intend to accomplish by visiting the home?
6. What follow-up to the visit will there be?

The hardest part of making home visits is deciding to do it; with conviction and practice, they become easier to manage. Home visits have a vital place in teaching and learning.

William W. Wayson writes:

> Home visits dispel myth, hearsay, and racial generalizations; they give the teachers an experiential knowledge of the child's environment.
>
> The teacher can help dispel negative feelings toward the school and teachers by exposing parents to a positive, concerned teacher. He becomes a person and often a friend and confidant when seen outside the school setting.
>
> Perhaps more importantly, home visits give the child a feeling that he and his family are important to the teacher. The child learns that his teacher and his parents share common goals for him and will work toward achieving them.[4]

In Conclusion

Teachers concerned with meeting the educational needs of their students know they can be most effective in helping students learn if they and the students' parents (or guardians) work together.

Working together involves more than just telling the parents that things are going well (or not going well) for students. It requires parents and teachers to sit down together as partners and plan ways for providing the best possible classroom and out-of-class experiences for students.

In many school districts around the United States, there are the scheduled parent-teacher organization meetings. At other times, teachers hold regular conferences with parents to report on pupil progress. Through these programs, parents occasionally see each other and teachers; but the occasions are far too rare and permit too little in-depth discussion.

With the advent of school desegregation, a large percentage of minority students now are being taught by Caucasian teachers who do not live in the ghetto, barrio, or on the reservation. Although school desegregation was designed to bring people of different races together, it may have created a chasm between teachers of one racial or ethnic group and students of another. In order to bridge the chasm, teachers must make home visits. They cannot afford to do otherwise.

---

1. Ann T. Henderson, "Parents Are a School's Best Friends," *Phi Delta Kappan* 70 (October 1988): 148.

2. Joseph F. Callahan and Leonard H. Clark, *Introduction to American Education* (New York: Macmillan, 1983), p. 279.

3. Henderson, op. cit., pp. 149-51.

4. William W. Wayson, "Educating for Renewal in Urban Communities," *National Elementary Principal* 51 (April 1972): 15-16.

We will be able to achieve a just and prosperous society only when our schools ensure that everyone commands enough shared knowledge to be able to communicate effectively with everyone else.

E.D. Hirsch

Chapter 13
Communication About AIDS and Health Practices

There is one thing worse than not communicating. It is thinking you have communicated when you have not.
                                                        Edgar Dale

One request is made to all teachers: take action to impart instruction on Acquired Immune Deficiency Syndrome (AIDS).

A fairly large percentage of educators still feel that discussions about AIDS are for "other" people. AIDS instruction is *long* overdue in most classrooms. AIDS is too big and too powerful an issue for it to be someone else's problem.

Most fears are caused by ignorance. Teachers and students must be willing to learn all there is to know about AIDS; the disease is the worst kind of killer.

It is particularly important that minority students be informed of the tragic consequences of promiscuous and unprotected sex and unsafe drug use. Too often, minority students are unknowingly victims of dangerous sex and drug practices, practices that often do not allow their users a second chance. Several national reports highlight that the incidence of AIDS is higher for minority populations on a percentage basis than for other populations.

Do not assume that your students know about AIDS — *tell them.* Communicate the need for them to abstain from unsafe sex and non-prescribed drug use.

Minority students, like all other students, appear to be at risk because they do not make informed health decisions. Although many know how AIDS is contracted, they may not know how to prevent AIDS or any of the other widespread sexually transmitted diseases.

Other health risks are presented by students who use illegal drugs, smoke cigarettes, or have poor diet habits. Health experts conservatively estimate that millions of teenagers smoke cigarettes. It also has been noted that smoking is declining among adolescent males but not among females.

As programs about AIDS and contemporary health practices are developed, it is very important to include parents in the planning and implementation phases. Parental involvement improves learning for most students, but it is especially important that parents of at-risk and minority students be active in working with the schools in applying such special programs beyond the classroom.

Parents who are poor or undereducated may face special barriers to involvement, but these barries can be overcome when schools and parents work together in bringing about improved communication to students with regard to the perils of AIDS and other negative health practices.

The key to success is communication. This is vital not only for the improved educational outcomes schools desire but also for the schools, parents, students, and others to work together to ensure that safe health practices are carried out by the students.

How many a man has dated
a new era in his life from
the reading of a book?

Henry David Thoreau

Chapter 14
Reading: The "Basic" Basic Skill

Education aims to expand, amplify, deepen and to refine the quality and continuity of one's experiences, to extend each person's radius of concern.

Edgar Dale

A large percentage of minority youth experience serious difficulty in mastering the traditional reading curriculum that is offered to them. For several environmental reasons, minority students progressively fall behind middle-class white students in reading ability as well as in verbal and mathematical ability with each successive grade level completed.

The problem of non-achievement of minority students in reading begins in their early years, even before entering kindergarten. There is evidence that many of them receive insufficient intellectual or cultural stimulation in the home.

Research indicates that the basic tools leading to successful reading in school are found in the home before the students enter school. Ideally, parents should provide their children with books and other reading materials. However, in some homes this is not possible. Parents are either undereducated and are not committed to this idea or they lack the financial resources for books and other materials that stimulate reading. This early deprivation leads to deficiencies evident in minority children's socioeducational development.

The testing of minority students' reading skills often is incorrectly evaluated by teachers who are unfamiliar with students' language and cultural orientation. Although many teachers may not ever reach a full understanding of their students' orientation, there is no reason why they can not be aware that this phenomenon exists.

Reading success is based on having materials that are relevant to students regardless of their ethnic or racial affiliation. This is not to say that all materials should have an ethnic basis. But some of them should be written by authors who are sensitive to the culture from which minority students come.

Minority students, like all students, like to read about experiences to which they can relate. Illustrations, familiar community settings, and characters depicting minorities enable these students to identify easily with the learning materials. But in order to avoid presenting a distorted picture, instructional materials involving middle-class, suburban, rural, and international experiences also must be included among minority students' reading materials.

The teacher should stress drills and overall comprehension on a daily basis. If group competition does not stifle the incentive of students to read, provide awards for those who read to predetermined achievement levels. If the class contains remedial learners, reading materials must be secured to suit their needs and interests. These materials may include films, filmstrips, tapes, records, audio/video cassettes, and the many computer programs that are available for teaching reading to remedial students.

Minority students must be taught to read well. Reading is the most basic of the basic skills; and without a firm and solid foundation in reading, the student's progress and other academic activities will be hampered. Even though many courses and disciplines are taught in the curriculum of the school, reading must be the mainstay.

Motivation is the key to reading. Without the proper motivation, many students will not develop adequate reading skills. Some find reading distasteful; others find it a chore because they have not developed a fondness for the printed page. Students can succeed at reading; but to do this, they must be afforded plenty of reading practice. Practice for reading is the "basic" basic skill.

*Education makes a people easy to
lead, but difficult to drive; easy to
govern, but impossible to enslave.*

—Lord Brougham

Chapter 15
Athletics and NCAA Proposition 48

The nice thing about teamwork
is that you always have others on your side.
Margaret Carty

Black athletes have been affected most by National Collegiate Athletic Association (NCAA) rules setting minimum academic standards for athletes, according to an Associated Press survey (September 1988).

The survey examined 274 high school recruits who were barred in 1988 from intercollegiate athletics by the NCAA standards known as Proposition 48. Of the athletes whose racial background could be determined, 86.8 percent were black.

Proposition 48 requires recruits to score at least 700 out of a possible 1600 on the Scholastic Aptitude Test, or 15 out of 36 on the American College Test. The rule also requires at least a 2.0 high school grade point average in 11 mandatory courses.

The fallout from a rule of this nature is predictable: it has its champions as well as critics. From a pragmatic standpoint, however, Proposition 48 is a rule that should have been in place many years ago. The problem is that: 1) black students may not have been exposed to college preparatory courses in high school; 2) students may not have taken the ACT and SAT seriously; and 3) a cavalier attitude held by some student-athletes may have led them to believe that athletic prowess, regardless of their academic skills, would gain them college admission.

Critics of standardized tests argue that the tests are culturally biased in favor of high school students from white, middle-class backgrounds.

They also charge that the tests are poor indicators of which students are likely to succeed in college. For these reasons, in their view, black students should not have to pass standardized tests to enter college and participate in athletic events.

Contrary to what these critics may argue, mathematics is mathematics, science is science, language arts is language arts, and writing is writing. Either the students know or do not know the information to respond to the questions on the test. There really is no black, white, brown, yellow, or red mathematics. Test items represent the universal content of known disciplines.

Minority students can succeed at anything they desire. They also are quite capable of passing standardized examinations. But some of them have built up a fear of examinations. Rather than developing skills to take a test the way they develop skills to shoot a basketball, run track, or play football, many deny their ability to pass a test by implying that it is something that only white people do well.

There is no use in belaboring the point as to why some minority students fear standardized examinations, as this will not improve their scores on the ACT or the SAT. What teachers of minority students and athletes need to do is to insist that they spend as much time in their textbooks as they do on the athletic field and in the gym. Teachers are also going to have to help minority students develop test taking skills and show them how to use the items on standardized examinations to their advantage. There is nothing magic about the SAT or ACT.

In order for minority athletes to escape the wrath of Proposition 48 and all of the sting that it puts into their educational future, they must start passing the required examinations. Teachers must help them to succeed by drilling them in course content. They must then give them practice on how to analyze problems and understand the various formats on standardized examinations. *That* is what Proposition 48 demands.

Much education today is monumentally ineffective. All too often we are giving young people cut flowers when we should be teaching them to grow their own plants.

John W. Gardner

Chapter 16
Minority Students:
Why Wait for Them to Fail?

Good teachers may cost more,
but poor teachers cost the most.
Anonymous

In some ways, the 1980s are the best of years and also the worst of years for minority students. The 1980s have seen a dramatic increase in education reform efforts, marked by the enactment of numerous initiatives that have turned into reform legislation in such states as South Carolina, Arkansas, Mississippi, and Indiana.

Teachers in America's schools know more today than teachers during any other period on *how* to teach. Yet there seems to be good reason to believe that what they know does not enable them to truly understand about reaching youngsters, especially minority learners and their various needs, both personal and educational.

Each year, according to the Joint Council on Economic Education, student dropouts cost the U.S. between $60 billion and $223 billion. By conservative estimates, these numbers do not account for all the money that is spent on welfare programs that support dropouts or on crime awareness and prevention programs. Keeping minority students in school costs money; but it will cost a lot more if they drop out of school.

Each day, teachers should present their students planned, sequenced, meaningful, and well-researched lessons. These lessons must be planned for individual and collective student needs.

Teachers must make a point of providing their students homework assignments that complement instructional objectives. These assignments should be such that students realize that homework is an extension of their in-class involvements. By all means, homework should be treated as importantly as regular instruction. Students should be accountable for completing their homework. If need be, parents should sign the homework.

Valuable class time should not be wasted on trivial or unimportant classroom pursuits. You, as a teacher, owe your students the maximum amount of learning time each day.

Communicate to your students that they *can* learn and that you *expect* them to learn. Remember to express a sincere respect for good work, especially by minority students. Single them out for praise that is relevant and appropriate.

You must effectively individualize instruction for all learners, the high achievers as well as those whose cognitive needs are dependent on prolonged personal and instructional interaction. The keys to success in this area are materials. Learner-directed and learner-corrected materials must provide the greater part of the remediation work in any classroom. Very few teachers can simultaneously present 25 to 30 individual exercises and presentations to as many students; materials can. To the fullest extent, promote John Dewey's philosophy: "Children learn by doing."

Booker T. Washington said it best when he wrote:

> Few things help an individual more than to place responsibility upon him, and to let him know that you trust him.

Washington's philosphy is as true today as it was at the beginning of this century. An effective teacher stimulates learning; and if learning proceeds from action, ample opportunity must be provided for learners to be engaged in the active pursuit of knowledge for themselves. Trust them; believe in their effort; provide the support systems they need to succeed. More often than not, your expectations will be realized when you place the responsibility for learning upon students.

Teachers who produce high quality learning differ from one another as much as the students with whom they interact. The element that effective teachers share is that they nurture and provide learning opportunities for students who are entrusted to them.

Even the greatest teaching performances can be improved. Teachers, too, can achieve peak performances. What do Bill Cosby, Cher, Ervin "Magic" Johnson, Ronald Reagan, John McEnroe, and others like them have in common, other than outstanding success in their fields?

Each possesses a high degree of self-esteem;

Each works in cooperation with others to achieve his or her goals;

Each is goal-oriented and directed to results; and

Each understands the importance of change and adaptability in his or her life.

Minority students are a great resource. Their success in school is vitally important. Good teachers are able to help them achieve that. Minority students must not fail!

The basis for the school's acceptability in the community must be demonstrated commitment to the well-being of the children it serves. That commitment must be demonstrated in actions understood by ghetto residents, if not by the larger community. It shines out of daily relationships with the child and community far more clearly than it resounds from pious statements.

William W. Wayson

Chapter 17
Teaching: No Pain, No Gain

Teaching is the art of guiding, of leading students toward a goal. It should not involve dictating particular ideas or behavior. Teaching includes presenting material to students and allowing them to draw their own conclusions.[1] It brings students to greater levels of awareness.

Most teachers never know how successful their teaching efforts are. They must give their best in trying to realize the goals and objectives they have set for their students. Sometimes the task of teaching becomes a painful job with only temporary relief in sight.

To be a teacher requires an extraordinary amount of stamina as well as personal, emotional, and intellectual commitment. According to Richard Celeste, Governor of Ohio:

> A teacher must have the energy of a harnessed volcano, the efficiency of an adding machine, the memory of an elephant, the understanding of a psychiatrist, the wisdom of Solomon, the tenacity of a spider . . . the decisiveness of a general . . . the diplomacy of an ambassador.[2]

Teaching can be painful. It requires thorough preparation to become a teacher. Teaching may be summed up as 10 percent inspiration, 5 percent motivation, and about 85 percent perseverance. The one thing teachers want from teaching is a winning combination for success; but in the process, they may feel defeated at times. Those who get up and dust themselves off are the true professionals.

While students are expected to remain in school until graduation, the dropout rate in American secondary schools averages between 25 percent and 30 percent. The secondary school dropout rate may be higher for some minorities. The irony of this is that while teachers must pay attention to students who come to class daily and are motivated to learn and succeed, they must also seek ways to bring back the students who are not in school. While teaching facts, numbers, logic, history, science, and the basic skills, in the back of many teachers' minds are those students who are not in the class: the dropouts, pushouts, and (soon-to-be) leftouts.

Who are the leftouts? The leftouts are the students who will not be awarded a high school diploma after twelve years in school because they failed to pass an exit examination. They receive a mere certificate of attendance for their efforts.

It is conjecture at this point what the certificate of attendance will mean to employers, college and university admission officers, educators, and most of all to students who have been awarded one. Will it be possible for certificate of attendance holders to earn a high school diploma once they are able to pass the Comprehensive Test of Basic Skills (CTBS) or its equivalent?

The worst pain of all is confronting the home and community where indifference to students, especially minority students, reigns supreme. Some students are so far behind in their studies that they should be in school year round. Also a detriment to education is when students are forced to be out of school because the educators are on strike (for whatever reason) or when parents do not support the educational needs of their children.

------

1. Marilyn Kowilsky and Lory Quaranta, *Effective Teaching* (Glenview, Ill.: Scott, Foresman and Company, 1987), p. 155.

2. Comments in a lecture delivered by Governor Celeste.

The number of homeless families with children increased during 1986 and 1987. According to a 26-city survey conducted by the U.S. Conference of Mayors, two-thirds of the people seeking emergency food were parents with children, as were one-third of those seeking shelter. The average increase in homeless families was 32 percent, with an increase as high as 144 percent in Charleston, South Carolina, and 75 percent in Providence, Rhode Island.

U.S. Conference of Mayors
Reported by *Learning* 17 (April 1988), p. 13

Chapter 18
Teachers Are Their Students' Keepers

Programs designed to increase school safety and decrease student drug dependence are urgently needed in the schools. In addition to safety and health factors, such programs could conceivably encourage students, especially the troubled ones, not to quit school before they graduate.

Special programs of this nature need the support of community groups in order to succeed; the schools cannot handle the accompanying fiscal and logistical commitments alone. School officials, social service agencies, churches, juvenile court officials, the Chamber of Commerce, and local police and sheriff's departments must be made to understand the necessity of these programs. With this understanding, greater commitments (financial and otherwise) can be encouraged to help develop programs that have the potential to curb activities that detract from educational courses.

Minority students are some of the hardest hit with respect to drug dependence. For this reason, school personnel, social service agencies, and law enforcement officials must share information with each other about drug dependence and its consequences. And because of their unique role in society, schools must help students deal with such illegal activities as drug abuse. Since adolescence tends to be stressful personally, socially, and emotionally for a high percentage of young people, the ultimate goal of such programs is to reach them before they are fully or badly affected by counterproductive behavioral patterns.

It is widely accepted that adolescents with difficulties who are properly assisted (through programs) by educators and law enforcement officials have a stronger potential to remain in school, graduate, and successfully enter adult life. If educators and their allies do not work together to assist today's young people with their problems, the likelihood is great for many that they will turn to crime, drugs, and other anti-social behaviors.

There are national programs to study conditions that are caused by student misbehavior. These programs, though varied in scope and purpose, serve as models for schools and community agencies to follow. The U.S. Justice Department and Pepperdine University in Los Angeles have an abundance of data on the nation's schools and the costs that result from damage to them by wayward students, as well as the responses of communities to these students' actions.

The National School Safety Center in Washington, D.C., also has data on safety measures that schools and community agencies must employ to reduce instances of student misbehavior and recommends effective ways to rid schools and communities of the conditions that foster student misbehavior. Student misbehavior costs millions of dollars in property damage annually and takes a toll on peoples' lives. The conditions that foster misbehavior in the classroom must be dealt with if the next generation is to enjoy a way of life based on respect, human decency, good ethics and, most of all, respect for self.

Where do teachers come into the picture? Outside the home, during a school year teachers have the most significant single contact with students. They are able to observe students on a daily basis. Teachers often are able to detect actions and attitudes that can lead to student misbehavior.

While teachers are not encouraged to take corrective or remedial action into their own hands, they must ask themselves: "What should my attitude be on what I saw or heard? To whom do I report these matters? Is it really my business to assess whether what I heard or saw may get someone into trouble or cause violence or the destruction of property?"

Teachers must be personally and professionally concerned with any student activities that could cause problems for themselves or anyone else. Teachers must be willing to inform a principal or supervisor about what they have heard. It is a teacher's responsibility to assess everything that goes on in the classroom or the school. Teaching involves more than just imparting information to students; it also requires correcting situations that need correcting and providing mature and professional leadership when leadership is needed. To paraphrase the Bible, "Teachers are their students' keepers."

We can teach so that our students feel inferior, or so as to help them think better of themselves.

Anonymous

Chapter 19
Praise, Encouragement, and Feedback in Instruction

Go forward, straight ahead. There are no limits on your life but those barricades you build yourself.
Rod McKuen, 1980

A teacher shows high regard for his students by providing them with honest feedback on their work. This indicates to students that the teacher has devoted time and made a commitment to assessing and evaluating their work. Carl Rogers writes:

> I hypothesize that growth and change are more likely to occur the more that the counselor is experiencing a warm, positive, acceptant attitude toward what is in the client.[1]

Too often teachers forget the power of praise and constructive criticism in instruction. Honest praise of students is an important tool in motivation. Students need to know that teachers have a positive attitude toward them. There is solid evidence in research on learning that students with a positive self-concept learn more efficiently. Verbal praise from teachers remains an external source of encouragement for student performance.[2]

Minority students need to be encouraged to do well in school and in life. Teachers should use praise that is sincere and will serve students. The use of praise is a powerful tool for teachers.

The following are additional skills teachers working with minority students may develop to serve them well:

1. *Avoid cajoling or flattery to persuade students to do something.*

2. *Avoid moralizing.* Moralizing has the effect of reinforcing the very behavior we moralize against. Minority students tend to tune out teachers who moralize.

3. *Avoid making deals with students to curtail undesired behavior.* Example: Several students have been disrupting classroom activity. You, the teacher, are strongly tempted to negotiate a "deal." Don't.

4. *Avoid responding to student challenges or tests of will; rather, show interest in students' interests, concerns, and knowledge.* Example: A student challenges you, refusing to work on an academic task. Many times such angry refusals from students are cases of displacement, in which the student reacts to the teacher as if he were someone else.[3]

It is strongly suggested that teachers of minority students read Herbert L. Foster's *Ribbin', Jivin', and Playin' the Dozens* (Cambridge, Mass.: Ballinger Publishing Company, 1974) to help them understand the lifestyles and educational idiosyncrasies of a large percentage of minority students. At the same time, it must be kept in mind that all minority students do not require educational strategies and techniques that are different from those provided to non-minority students.

There are thousands of minority students (Blacks, Chicanos, Native Americans, Hispanics, Asians, and others) who are far superior to white students with respect to performance in the classroom and success later in life. However, these students are the exceptions rather than the rule. There also are untold numbers of minority students who succeed well in school and score very well on achievement tests because they have the support of their families and are intrinsically motivated to succeed in school and in life. These minority students are likely to succeed regardless of conditions in the schools they attend or their teachers' attitudes.

According to Professor James B. Boyer, a pioneer in the field of multi-ethnic and interracial understanding:

> [There are] learners from limited-income families; and these include those whose family income is considerably limited when compared to most other families in America or in a given locality. They are children who come from economically poor homes and whose lifestyles differ markedly because of factors associated with family income.[4]

Success in school and school achievement often are tied directly to economics. For many minority students, the poor economic conditions in which they are raised severely affect their ability to learn. As teachers develop and foster relationships with students, the latter will sense that teachers genuinely care about them and their educational progress.

It is incumbent on teachers to go the "extra mile" in providing for the education of all minority students. Through diligent effort, a sizable portion of the next generation of minority students will be able to overcome the economic and educational barriers that limited their parents' and grandparents' success in school.

Reinforcers in Teaching

Teachers also need to have the kinds of verbal (and written) reinforcers at their disposal that stir minority students to action.

On the surface, minority students may appear to be passive learners who are not receptive to normal classroom reinforcers that teachers use to encourage students to do well in school. Teachers may sometimes feel that minority students do not wish to be reinforced.

On the contrary, minority students need the same praise, feedback, and reinforcement that other students receive. Minority students, for whatever reasons, may not receive much of any of these in other areas of their life. They often are subjected to a good deal of criticism, some of which may be deserved. Nevertheless, if they constantly hear such commentary, they may begin to "tune out" advice and helpful criticism altogether.

If the teacher speaks the language (or dialect) of minority students, this language should be employed. English is not the only language that is available to the teacher in using written and verbal reinforcers. Select from the following list of reinforcers those that will best facilitate learning and achievement for all students. Do it on a consistent basis.

> That's right!
> You've just about got it.
> That's it!
> I knew you could do it.
> Very good.
>
> That's quite an improvement.
> You make it look easy.
> One more time and you'll have it.
> That's the way.
> Right on!

Keep up the good work.
PERFECT!
That's the best ever.
This is first-class work.
A+

You're really going to town now!
TREMENDOUS!
Much better!
You did that very well.
You must have been practicing.

Your writing skills make me proud.
Hey, you are on a roll now.
Keep it up.
You certainly did well today.
Good thinking.

The way you are going, the Ph.D. degree is yours to grab.
Keep on trying.
Good job, _____.
You remembered!
Good efforts.

---

1. Carl Rogers, "The Interpersonal Relationship: The Case of Guidance," *Harvard Educational Review* 32 (Fall 1962): 420.

2. Donald E. Orlosky, *Introduction to Education,* (Toronto: Charles E. Merrill, 1982), p. 277.

3. Ibid.

4. James B. Boyer, *Racial Integration and Learners from Limited Income Families* (Manhattan, Kan.: Mid-West Educational Associates, 1979), p.2.

Only the person who has faith in himself is able to be faithful to others.

Erich Fromm

Chapter 20
Postscript: Effective Teaching Success

Before success comes in any man's life, he is sure to meet with much temporary defeat, and, perhaps, some failure. When defeat overtakes a man, the easiest and most logical thing to do is to quit. That is exactly what the majority of men do.

Napolean Hill

Teaching is extremely hard work. It taxes energy and it takes emotional and physical tolls on the individual. But if one has the true desire to become an effective teacher, he or she can overcome the initial and, at times, very real failures a teacher will experience.

What is important in any teacher's life is that any desire to quit teaching be overcome. By all means, strive for teaching success and do not accept defeat. Promote a sense of commitment that permits you to realize what you thought was impossible.